# GRADES 4, 5 & 6

**Publisher** ................................................................. *Arthur L. Miley*

**Art Director** .................................................................. *Debbie Birch*

**Cover Design** ............................................................... *Gary Zupkas*

**Editor** ............................................................................ *Sandra J. Stone*
*with Grace Abbott*

**Production Coordinator** ........................................... *Valarie Fetrow*

**Illustrators** ................................................................... *Fran Kizer*
*Peter Demos*

**Proofreader** ................................................................. *Barbara Bucher*

THIS BOOK BELONGS TO

_____

Rainbow Books

*Copyright © 1999 • Tenth Printing*
Rainbow Books • P.O. Box 261129 • San Diego, CA 92196

#RB36182
ISBN 0-937282-77-4

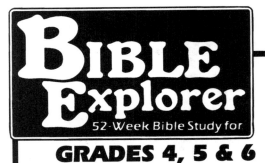

# For Parents

This *BIBLE EXPLORER 52-Week Bible Study* will help your junior-age child learn how to read and study God's Word, the Bible.

An exciting adventure story about two children, John and Isabel, who go on a sea voyage to find the New Land, will guide your child week by week through this enchanting Bible study. Your child will learn about Jesus, our Savior, and how to follow and obey God in daily activities.

They will learn what to do when they are afraid, and how to handle trouble when it comes. As John and Isabel learn they must obey the captain's orders, your child will learn how to follow God's rules, too. Memorization of key Bible verses is also emphasized and he or she will also be given the opportunity to accept Jesus Christ as his or her personal Savior.

Fun and interesting puzzles, pencil games and other exciting activities reinforce what the Bible teaches and shows your child how to apply the Bible teaching to daily life at home, school and with family and friends. The King James Version of the Bible is used throughout this book, but your child may read and memorize the verses from another Bible translation if you wish.

To make this study of God's Word most effective, you may want to read the Bible verses and lessons from this book with your child and thoughtfully talk with him or her about what he or she is learning, relating it to everyday events in your family. You or another adult should sign each page as your child completes it.

The program is designed to be completed over a 52-week period, or one year, but your child may go faster or slower as desired. Your child may record his or her progress through the book by coloring in the appropriate flag for each week he or she completes on the Adventure Map on page 4. Page 63 offers some practical suggestions for continuing to study and memorize God's Word after this study is completed.

### A Note to Teachers

This book is ideal for use in Sunday schools, children's church, "kids' clubs" and Christian schools because it combines an exciting Scripture-memorization program with solid Bible study, while providing challenging, fun activities which help the children grow spiritually. In addition, the BIBLE EXPLORER gets children started early in the habit of daily Bible study and memorization.

One book should be provided to each child so he or she may take the book home for daily Bible study. The child should be encouraged to bring his or her book to class each week for the teacher to review. Stickers to place on the completed page, or other incentives, could be given to the child for completing each weekly lesson. In Christian schools, the child may do one section or portion of the weekly lesson each day or complete the entire study in one day.

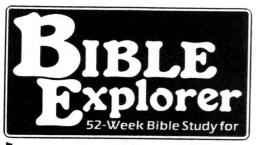

# Welcome Aboard!

How would you like to go on an exciting sea voyage?

It's easy! Your whole trip is right here inside this *Bible Explorer* book!

Your guides will be John and Isabel, two children just about your age. While you're traveling along with them, you will learn about God and His Word, the Bible.

For most boys and girls the trip through this book takes about 52 weeks, or one year. You might want to go faster or slower, and that's OK.

All along your trip you will encounter exciting puzzles, pencil games, and other activities to help you learn and study the Bible.

Here are some easy ways to make your trip the very best:

☐ Choose a special time each day to read and study the lesson for that week.

☐ Review the memory verse so by the end of the week, you will know the verse from memory.

☐ Put a check mark in the box in front of each activity as you complete it.

☐ When you have completed the whole lesson for the week, color in the correct flag on the Bible Explorer Adventure Map on page 4.

☐ Ask your mother or father or another adult to sign the bottom of each page before you go on to the next week.

☐ If you wish, you can color the picture of John and Isabel's ship, the *Explorer*, at the bottom of each page as you complete it.

**Get ready! Let's get started on this exciting adventure through the Bible!**

# Contents

# THE GREAT VOYAGE BEGINS

John and Isabel worked quickly to finish their chores in their Father's map-making shop by the sea. From the shop window they could see huge sailing ships come and go.

John and Isabel often stared out the window at the harbor. They daydreamed of the time they would set sail on their own great adventure.

Now along the horizon the children saw the faint glimmer of white sails. This could be the day!

Months earlier they signed on as cabin crew on the *Explorer*, a large sailing ship. Their father would sail with them, taking this opportunity to chart unexplored lands and update his maps.

Perhaps this was the *Explorer* coming into port, and their adventure was about to begin! As the ship drew nearer, John and Isabel anxiously watched. They recognized the magnificent sails towering over the long, wooden ship. The *Explorer* had arrived!

"I'll race you to the pier," shouted John to Isabel as he dashed out the door and along the busy harbor. Yes, their exciting voyage would soon begin!

This is just the beginning of an exciting adventure for you too. As you travel through this book with John and Isabel, you will explore God's Word, the Bible, and discover new truths to help you follow Christ and live for Him. Sometimes the journey will be hard, but along the way you will discover some great treasures to reward your faithful work.

Don't desert the ship or your friends John and Isabel, because you may miss some important treasures and discoveries!

When John and Isabel reached the pier, the *Explorer* was just docking, and the children waited impatiently for the captain to alight.

"Go home and pack your bag," the captain warned the children. "Tomorrow we sail for the New Land."

John and Isabel were very excited. They could hardly believe that they were really part of the *Explorer* crew. But they had made the decision to go, and now the time for their adventure had come!

**Your adventure with Jesus Christ must begin with your decision to follow Jesus Christ. Have you made this decision?**

## Memory Verse

☐ *"But as many as received Him, to them gave He power to become the sons of God, even to them that believe on His name."* John 1:12

## Study The Verse

☐ Circle these key words in the verse above: received, power, sons of God, believe.

## Study The Bible

☐ Read the following verses in your Bible. Match each verse with the correct thought.

John 1:12       Believe in Jesus Christ to be saved

John 3:16       Receive Jesus Christ to be God's child

Acts 16:31      Believe in Jesus Christ for eternal life

## Think About This

☐ What would your life be without Jesus?

_____  _____

Parent or adult signature     Date

# The Great Voyage Begins  WEEK 2

John and Isabel learned about this great voyage from their father. One day he came home from the pier and asked, "John and Isabel, would you like to go on a sea voyage?"

"Oh, yes, Father," both children cried. "Mother, can we go?"

After a little coaxing, Mother finally agreed to let the children experience this new adventure.

**How did you find out about Jesus Christ? Were you excited when you learned of Him?**

## Memory Verse

☐ *"And that from a child thou hast known the holy scriptures, which are able to make thee wise unto salvation through faith which is in Christ Jesus."*

2 Timothy 3:15

## Study The Verse

☐ Fill in the blanks.

*"And that from a _____ thou hast _____ the _____ _____ , which are able to make thee _____ unto _____ through _____ which is in _____ _____ ."*

## Study The Bible

☐ Read about the two people below. Write down who told them about Christ. What did they do when they heard about Jesus?

Philippian jailer (Acts 16:23-25)_____

_____

Ethiopian (Acts 8:26-39)_____

## Something To Do

☐ Write and send a thank you note to the person or persons who told you about Jesus. Or write a personal note to God thanking Him for sending Jesus to be your Savior; read the note to God in prayer.

_____    _____
Parent or adult signature                    Date

With their bags packed, John, Isabel and their father walked to the harbor. There they looked up at the *Explorer's* huge sails. These sails would capture the wind, and take them to places they had never seen before.

Just as the wind and sails empower the ship to move across the sea, so Jesus Christ gives you the power to become His child and to live a life of faith.

## Memory Verse

☐ Say John 1:12 again. See page 6.

## Study The Verse

☐ Write John 1:12 in your own words.

_____

_____

_____

_____

☐ Underline John 1:12 in your Bible.

## Study The Bible

☐ Read Acts 1:8-11. Answer these questions. In verse 8, what does Jesus promise you can receive?

_____

From whom can you receive it?_____What will it help you to do?_____

Write down three places you can be a witness for Jesus:

_____     _____     _____

## Think About This

☐ Could you live the Christian life without Jesus Christ in you and with you to help you? (Circle one)

    YES          NO

_____     _____
Parent or adult signature         Date

John, Isabel and their father boarded the Explorer. Their father introduced them to the captain whom they had met the day before when the ship docked. "Are you ready to help make this voyage a success?" he asked the children.

"Oh, yes, Sir!" the children both answered. "We will work hard and do our very best!"

**Christians should be committed to Christ just like John and Isabel are committed to their captain. Do you get as excited about Jesus as John and Isabel are about their voyage?**

## Memory Verse

☐ *"And thou shalt love the Lord thy God with all thy heart, and with all thy soul, and with all thy mind, and with all thy strength: this is the first commandment."*

Mark 12:30

## Study The Verse

☐ Circle the four phrases in the verse above which tell how we should love God.

## Study The Bible

☐ Read Mark 12:28-31. Answer these questions.

1. What is the first commandment?_____

2. What is the second commandment?_____

## Something To Do

☐ Express your love to God by spending time with Him in prayer each day this week. Each day you pray, circle or color in the picture of the praying hands below. Even after this week, make it a habit to pray each day.

_____     _____

Parent or adult signature                              Date

# The Great Voyage Begins  WEEK 5

Settled in their cabin, John and Isabel carefully unpacked their books. They were glad they had spent the previous months studying about ships, maps, sailing and the sea. These books would be helpful throughout the voyage.

**Studying God's Word, the Bible, is very important for Christians. God's Word tells us about Jesus Christ, and gives us direction for our lives.**

## Memory Verse

☐ *"Study to show thyself approved unto God, a workman that needeth not to be ashamed, rightly dividing the word of truth."*

2 Timothy 2:15

## Study The Verse

☐ Unscramble the following words and then circle them in the verse above.

nkrwoma _____    ytusd _____    rowd _____

dvopapre _____    hurtt _____

☐ Read the memory verse and 2 Timothy 3:15. The phrases "holy scriptures" and "word of truth" refer to the ___ ___ ___ ___ ___ .

## Study The Bible

☐ Read 2 Timothy 2:22-25. Write three things a Christian should do and the two things a Christian should not do.

A Christian should

1. _____
2. _____
3. _____

A Christian should not

1. _____
2. _____

## Think About This

☐ How would you feel if you did not have a Bible to study? What would you do if your Bible was taken away and you could not have another?

_____    _____
Parent or adult signature                          Date

Standing on deck, John and Isabel stared out over the wide ocean as the ship set sail. What great things would they see? They committed themselves to this voyage. They placed their lives in the captain's hands.

**Christians should commit their lives to Jesus Christ. This is God's will or what He wants you to do. You can trust Jesus Christ with your life, because He will do only what is best for you.**

## Memory Verse

☐ *"I beseech you therefore, brethren, by the mercies of God, that ye present your bodies a living sacrifice, holy, acceptable unto God, which is your reasonable service."*

Romans 12:1

## Study The Verse

☐ Define these words. Use a dictionary.

a. sacrifice_____

b. acceptable_____

## Study The Bible

☐ Read how God helped those who were committed to Him. Write what God did for each person. Then tell someone else about each person.

Noah (Read Genesis 6:5-8, 13, 14, 17, 21-23.):_____

Moses (Read Hebrews 11:23-29.):_____

Daniel (Read Daniel 6:10-12, 16-22.):_____

## Think About This

☐ How can you be more committed to God? What will you miss out on if your life is not committed to God?

_____     _____
Parent or adult signature                Date

Soon the captain introduced the children to the rest of the crew. Most of the crew had sailed with the captain before. The children listened to their tales of their sea voyages. They soon discovered that each person on board was dedicated to the captain. They all loved this wise man.

**A Christian's dedication to Christ must begin by giving all his love to Jesus. If we can't give God our love, do you think He is pleased with the things we do for Him?**

## Memory Verse

☐ Say Mark 12:30 again. See page 9.

## Study The Verse

☐ What does commandment mean?_____

_____

☐ Underline Mark 12:30 in your Bible.

## Study The Bible

☐ Read Mark 12:28-31 again. Answer these questions.

1. Why do you think God says we must love Him more than anyone else?_____

_____

2. Why is it important to God what you do with your mind and your body?_____

_____

## Think About This

☐ At the close of one day, think of three or four things you have done that day. Ask yourself, "Am I pleased with these actions? Is God pleased with them?"

_____     _____
Parent or adult signature                          Date

Back in the cabin, Isabel began to record all the events of the trip in her diary. Read what she wrote:

WE'VE BEGUN THE VOYAGE. IT'S SO EXCITING! OUR FIRST STOP IS THE ISLAND OF PLENTY TO PICK UP PROVISIONS.

With your heart committed to Christ, continue on your journey in God's Word. Learn all you can about God's provisions for you. When you accept Jesus as your personal Savior, you start on a spiritual journey. It is important to read God's Word, the Bible, and pray each day. God's Word is "food" for your spiritual life.

## Memory Verse

☐ Say Romans 12:1 again. See page 11.

## Study The Verse

☐ Underline Romans 12:1 in your Bible.

☐ What does this verse mean to you?_____

_____

## Study The Bible

☐ Jesus Christ sacrificed His life for your salvation. He became your *provision* for sin. Read about Jesus' care for you in Hebrews 13:5b. What did Jesus say?

_____

## Something To Do

☐ Say these verses again until you know them by heart:

    ☐ John 1:12    ☐ Mark 12:30
    ☐ 2 Timothy 3:15    ☐ 2 Timothy 2:15

_____    _____

Parent or adult signature          Date

# SMOOTH SAILING

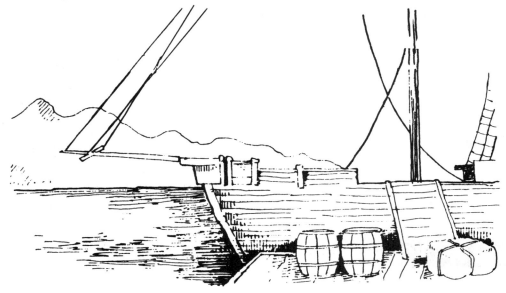

While the *Explorer* stopped at the Island of Plenty for supplies, John and Isabel explored the interesting places along the harbor.

Near one of the shops, John and Isabel met the captain. "Are you enjoying being part of the *Explorer* crew?" he asked.

"Yes," John said, "but we are a little tired of doing the same jobs. And, do we have to obey all the ship's rules all the time?"

"Can't we do some more exciting jobs and skip a few rules now and then?" asked Isabel.

"Be faithful in the little jobs I give you," the captain explained, "and soon you will be ready for more difficult, exciting duties. As for the ship's rules, you must obey them all the time. This is for your safety and the safety of the crew."

John and Isabel assured the captain that they would be obedient and do their best work so this voyage would be a smooth-sailing success.

God gives responsibilities, rules and directions to His children. They are written in the Bible. As you continue to grow in Christ, God will give you more and more responsibilities. God wants you to be faithful in what you do now. He wants you to be obedient to His rules (commands) because He knows His rules will help you live successfully for Him.

# Smooth Sailing  WEEK 9

Since the beginning of this trip, John and Isabel have been committed to the voyage and the Captain. They would not even think of joining another ship's crew or deserting the captain. Their allegiance is to him.

In the Ten Commandments, God gives us the rules or commands for our lives. God's first command is to put Him first in our lives. Your love and allegiance belong to Him above all else.

## Memory Verse

☐ *"Thou shalt have no other gods before Me. Thou shalt not make unto thee any graven image."*

Exodus 20:3, 4a

## Study The Verse

☐ Notice that God's name always begins with a capital letter. That is because He is the only true God. Circle all the words that refer to God.

Notice the small "g" on the word "gods" in the verse above. This word does not refer to the one true God, it refers to things or people we may worship or love in place of the one true God, our Heavenly Father.

## Study The Bible

☐ Read Exodus 20:1-6. Answer these questions.

1. Who is speaking in these verses? (vs. 1) _____

2. What are two things God commands us not to do.

    a. _____

    b. _____

3. To whom will God show mercy (kindness)? _____

## Something To Do

☐ Make a list of some things people give first place in their lives instead of God. (Examples: money, friends, clothes, etc.)

_____    _____

Parent or adult signature                Date

One day John and Isabel heard a crewman talking badly about the captain. How could this person say such bad things about their wonderful captain? John and Isabel were very sad.

You may have a friend you love very much. If someone else says unkind things about your friend it makes you feel sad. That's because you are loyal to your friend. God wants your loyalty too. Sometimes this is called "allegiance" or "devotion."

## Memory Verse

☐ "Thou shalt not take the name of the LORD thy God in vain . . . Remember the sabbath day, to keep it holy."
Exodus 20:7a, 8

## Study The Verse

God commands that His name not be used in vain or as a swear word. Christians should never do this, of course, because of their love and respect for God and His rules.

☐ Fill in the boxes with the correct words from the verses.

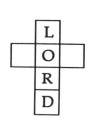
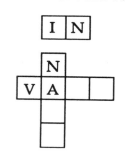
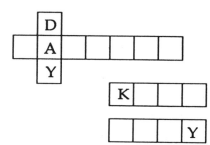

## Study The Bible

☐ Read Romans 10:9 & 13. What two things do these verses say you should use your mouth for?
_____

☐ Read Exodus 20:8-11. What does God say to do on the Sabbath? Why?_____
_____

## Think About This

☐ Do you think swearing and telling someone that Jesus is our Lord should come out of the same mouth? (Circle one.)

YES          NO

_____          _____
Parent or adult signature                        Date

# Smooth Sailing  WEEK 11

Even though John and Isabel are sailing with the captain, they are still under their father's authority. They must be obedient to the captain and to their father as well.

**God commands you to obey your parents. This is one of His rules for successful Christian living.**

## Memory Verse

☐ *"Honour thy father and thy mother: that thy days may be long upon the land which the LORD thy God giveth thee."*

Exodus 20:12

## Study The Verse

☐ What does *honor* mean? Use a dictionary._____

☐ What does the verse say is the result of honoring your parents?

_____

## Study The Bible

☐ Read Ephesians 6:1-3. Fill in the blanks.

Ephesians 6:1 says for you to _____ your _____ because this is _____ .

Ephesians 6:2 says that to "honor your father and mother" is the first commandment with a promise. What is the promise for honoring your parents? (vs. 3)

_____

Have you been obeying and honoring your parents? How long has it been since you thanked your mother or father for all the things they do for you?

## Something To Do

☐ Make a list of ways in which you may show your parents that you love, honor and respect them. Include things that would show your parents by your actions how you feel about them (for example, doing a job without being asked).

☐ Take time now to do one of the things on your list. Then try each day to show your parents that you do love, honor and respect them.

_____     _____
Parent or adult signature                          Date

One of the captain's rules was "Do not hurt one another." God has several commands to us about not hurting each other. Here are two of these commands.

**SHIP'S RULES**

DO NOT HURT ONE ANOTHER

## Memory Verse

☐ *"Thou shalt not kill. Thou shalt not commit adultery."* Exodus 20:13, 14

## Study The Verse

☐ Circle the correct answers.

In Exodus 20:13 God means we should not kill
   a. plants          b. people          c. animals

In Exodus 20:14 God means that married people should
   a. not love their relatives
   b. not care for others
   c. love each other and not fall in love with anyone else

## Study The Bible

☐ Read about David's sin in 2 Samuel 11:2, 3, 6, 14-17, 26, 27. Answer these questions.

1. What two commandments did David disobey?

   _____

   _____

2. How did God feel about David's sin? (2 Samuel 11:27)

   _____

   _____

## Think About This

☐ What would the world be like if everyone disobeyed God's rules?

_____          _____
Parent or adult signature                Date

John and Isabel were awakened in the middle of the night by some loud noises. They peeked out the cabin door. The captain was in the hall with some men.

"What happened?" the children called out.

"Someone has stolen some of the gold coins out of the ship's treasury," the captain explained. This money was to be used to buy food for the trip home. The man's stealing caused a lot of trouble and could have endangered the crew if he had not been caught. Not only did the man steal but he also lied. He said his cabin mate committed the crime.

**God has two more rules He wants you to follow. Read these.**

## Memory Verse

☐ *"Thou shalt not steal. Thou shalt not bear false witness against thy neighbour."*
Exodus 20:15, 16

## Study The Verse

☐ What does it mean to steal?_____

_____

☐ Circle the words in the verses above which mean "lie."

## Study The Bible

☐ Read Proverbs 12:22. What does it say about lying?_____

☐ Read Ephesians 4:28. What does this verse say about a thief?_____

## Think About This

☐ What does God say? Circle the correct statements.

Do not steal money   Do not tell lies about your friends.
Do not steal from your parents. Do not steal.
Do not lie.     Do not lie about what you have been doing.

☐ Have you ever stolen or lied? Ask Jesus to forgive you and help you to obey His commands from now on.

_____ _____
Parent or adult signature     Date

Coveting means to want what someone else has — not just wishing you had one like it, but wanting theirs — so they couldn't have it!

The captain gave Isabel a small wooden ship. John was jealous and covetous. He wanted that ship for himself. For a whole week John was mean to Isabel because she had a ship and he didn't. He felt rotten inside.

Finally John decided that coveting was not a happy way to live. He told Isabel he was sorry for treating her badly. She forgave him and shared the tiny ship. John felt a lot better!

**God does not want Christians to covet. God knows this is not a happy way to live and it can lead to doing other sinful things.**

## Memory Verse

☐ *"Thou shalt not covet thy neighbour's house . . . nor any thing that is thy neighbour's."*
Exodus 20:17

## Study The Verse

☐ What does this verse mean to you?_____

_____

_____

## Study The Bible

☐ Read the story in Matthew 20:20-24 and the story in Matthew 19:16-22. The first story tells about two disciples who wanted to make sure they had the best place in heaven. The second story is about a young man who wanted to keep all his money.

Which of these do you think was coveting?_____

## Think About This

☐ Is there a difference between coveting and just wanting something?

☐ Ask God to help you not to covet anything.

_____          _____
Parent or adult signature                      Date

John and Isabel decided that the best way to be obedient to all the rules was first to know them. Carefully they studied the list of rules.

**God wants us to know His rules or commands and then to obey them. If we don't know God's rules, there is no way we can be sure to obey them.**

## Memory Verse

☐ Review all God's commands you have learned. Practice saying them until you know them by heart.

1. *"Thou shalt have no other gods before Me.*
2. *Thou shalt not make unto thee any graven image . . .*
3. *Thou shalt not take the name of the LORD thy God in vain . . .*
4. *Remember the sabbath day, to keep it holy . . .*
5. *Honour thy father and thy mother: that thy days may be long upon the land which the LORD thy God giveth thee.*
6. *Thou shalt not kill.*
7. *Thou shalt not commit adultery.*
8. *Thou shalt not steal.*
9. *Thou shalt not bear false witness against thy neighbor.*
10. *Thou shalt not covet thy neighbour's house . . . nor any thing that is thy neighbour's."*

Exodus 20:3, 4a, 7a, 8, 12, 13, 14, 15, 16, 17

## Study The Verse

☐ Underline these verses in your Bible.

## Study The Bible

☐ Match each verse to the correct thought.

Psalm 119:11            God's commands make us wise

Psalm 119:98           We should love God's commandments above gold

Psalm 119:127         Knowing God's Word can keep us from sin

## Something To Do

☐ Make a collage of headlines from newspapers or magazines that show how people break these commandments. Write the commandments on the collage. Hang the collage in your room to help you remember to *obey* God's commands.

_____   _____

Parent or adult signature        Date

John and Isabel's father did a lot of things to make this trip possible for them. He worked very hard to have enough money to go on the trip and provide John and Isabel with clothing and food. He did this because he loved them.

John and Isabel appreciate their father and all the kind and loving things he does for them. They want to obey him because they love him.

**You should want to obey God because you love Him and are thankful for all the things He has done for you.**

## Memory Verse

☐ *"What? know ye not that your body is the temple of the Holy Ghost which is in you, which ye have of God, and ye are not your own? For ye are bought with a price: therefore glorify God in your body, and in your spirit, which are God's."*

1 Corinthians 6:19, 20

## Study The Verse

God, through the Holy Spirit, lives in you. You should want to make sure that God is pleased with all you do.

☐ Answer these questions.

1. Who lives inside Christians?_____

2. To whom do Christians belong?_____

3. With what should you glorify (honor) God?_____

## Study The Bible

☐ Study the 10 Commandments on **page 21**. On a separate piece of paper, write two of the commandments in your own words.

## Think About This

☐ Do you love God? Do your actions show that you love God and belong to Him?

_____     _____
Parent or adult signature                        Date

Early one morning, John and Isabel heard someone calling "Land Ho! Land Ho!" The Island of Lost Treasures was sighted. Now the smooth-sailing *Explorer* would soon anchor in a tiny cove where friendly natives waited to greet them. The *Explorer* crew was known throughout the island as kind and trustworthy men. John and Isabel wanted to be sure their actions lived up to the *Explorer* crew's reputation.

**Christians belong to Jesus Christ. He lives inside us through the Holy Spirit. We should want to bring honor to Him by our actions and obedience to His commands.**

## Memory Verse

☐ Say 1 Corinthians 6:19, 20 again. See page 22.

## Study The Verse

☐ Define these words. Use a dictionary.

temple_____

glorify_____

☐ Underline 1 Corinthians 6:19, 20 in your Bible.

## Study The Bible

☐ The Ten Commandments are things God says we *should* and *should not* do. God also gives us more commands of things we *should* do. Read each verse below. Write what God says we should do.

1 John 3:23:     1. _____     2. _____

Ephesians 4:32: _____

2 Timothy 2:15: _____

## Something To Do

☐ Say the Ten Commandments again. See page 21.

_____        _____

Parent or adult signature                    Date

# THE ISLAND OF LOST TREASURES

At last! The Island of Lost Treasures. What exciting adventures would John and Isabel find there? Legends told how several ships landed there filled with gold and jewels. They buried their treasure and returned to rough and angry seas. The ships were never seen again.

"All aboard!" called the captain. He was taking a small boat full of crew members to rest on this beautiful island. John and Isabel did not want to go ashore to rest or even play. They wanted to find buried treasure!

The Bible is God's treasure. It is filled with God's promises to His children. John and Isabel wanted very much to find treasure. They planned to dig and dig until they made a discovery. We need to "dig" into God's Word by studying it each day, to find the precious promise jewels God has for us.

As soon as John and Isabel reached the Island of Lost Treasures, they searched for just the right spot to dig. Under a palm tree near the shore seemed the perfect place to bury a treasure. They would begin digging there.

Jesus Christ is the source of the Christian's treasure. Your spiritual life begins when you accept Jesus as your personal Savior. He is the One Who will help you to find and understand God's Word.

## Memory Verse

☐ *"In Whom are hid all the treasures of wisdom and knowledge."*
Colossians 2:3

## Study The Verse

☐ Underline Colossians 2:3 in your Bible.

☐ This verse talks about Jesus Christ. What are the two treasures we find in Jesus?

1. _____     2. _____

## Study The Bible

☐ Read John 1:1-15, 29-36. Using information found in these verses, write a paragraph about Jesus Christ, the living Word.

## Think About This

☐ The Bible says in Matthew 6:21, *"For where your treasure is, there will your heart be also."* Is your treasure in Jesus?

_____     _____
Parent or adult signature              Date

John and Isabel started digging. It was hard work to dig in the sand, and soon John and Isabel were tired.

Then suddenly Isabel touched something hidden in the sand. She could hardly believe her eyes. There in the dirt was a large, red jewel.

"We did it!" John and Isabel shouted. "We found some treasure!" Excitedly they both began to dig deeper and faster.

**The first treasure we find in God's Word is love. Without God's love, Jesus would not have come to earth to die on the cross so He could be our Savior. God's love saves us from sin and God's love *helps* us to keep from sinning. What a precious treasure God's love is!**

## Memory Verse

☐ *"But God commendeth His love toward us, in that, while we were yet sinners, Christ died for us."*
Romans 5:8

## Study The Verse

☐ Unscramble these words from Romans 5:8.

ovle _____   rnisnes _____

ihCrst _____   deid _____

☐ Circle these words in the verse above.

## Study The Bible

☐ Read about God's love in Romans 8:37-39.

List 10 things that cannot separate us from Christ's love:

_____

_____

## Something To Do

☐ Write a story about God's protecting love. Use some ideas from Romans 8:37-39.

_____        _____
Parent or adult signature                          Date

"Look!" yelled John. "I found one, too!" The excitement was building. John pulled out a sparkling diamond. John and Isabel could not contain their happiness. They were jumping up and down for joy.

**Jesus Christ gives us joy. He tells us that He has come to give us a more abundant life — a life full of peace and happiness and joy.**

## Memory Verse

☐ *"Thou wilt show me the path of life: in Thy presence is fulness of joy; at Thy right hand there are pleasures for evermore."*

Psalm 16:11

## Study The Verse

☐ Write what Psalm 16:11 means in your own words.

_____

_____

_____

## Study The Bible

☐ Read the last part of Nehemiah 8:10. Finish this sentence:

God's joy gives us_____

☐ God gives us reason to have joy or *rejoice*. Today read Psalm 33 or Psalm 103. They are psalms of joy and praise. Write at least three reasons why we can rejoice in the Lord.

_____

_____

_____

## Think About This

☐ Bad things may happen all around us, but God gives us His joy and no one can take it away from us no matter what happens.

_____      _____
Parent or adult signature                    Date

John and Isabel were so excited about the hidden treasures they found that they could not dig anymore. They ran to find their father and the captain and tell them about this exciting discovery.

**God, in love, has saved us because Jesus died and rose again to become our Savior. He surrounds us in His love and gives us His joy. We should be excited about this and want to tell others about Him.**

## Memory Verse

☐ Say Romans 5:8 again. See page 26.

## Study The Verse

☐ Underline Romans 5:8 in your Bible.

☐ Did Christ die for us because we were good? Circle one.

     YES               NO

☐ Read Acts 16:31 and Mark 5:19. What two things do these verses tell us about what we should do because Jesus died for us:

_____

## Study The Bible

☐ Read the verses below. Write the one word which is common to all the verses: _____

    John 3:16             1 John 4:19
    Romans 5:8        2 Corinthians 13:11
    1 John 4:7          Ephesians 3:19

## Something To Do

☐ Read John 11:1-45. Illustrate this Bible story about Jesus' love and power in cartoon form. Use only the main parts of the story.

_____   _____

Parent or adult signature          Date

After John and Isabel told their father and the captain about the treasure they found, their father and the captain quickly returned with John and Isabel to the digging site. The excitement captured them all as they began to dig. John and Isabel had a satisfying peace in their hearts. They had discovered something wonderful and shared it with those they loved.

Just then their father found a string of pearls. What other exciting treasures waited to be found?

**God has given us His salvation, joy and peace. We should share these with other people so they can experience it too.**

## Memory Verse

☐ *"Peace I leave with you, My peace I give unto you: not as the world giveth, give I unto you. Let not your heart be troubled, neither let it be afraid."*

John 14:27

## Study The Verse

☐ Fill in the blanks.

*"Peace I _____ with _____ , My _____ I _____ unto you: not as the _____*

*giveth, _____ I unto you. Let not your _____ be _____ , neither let it be*

*_____ ."* John 14:27

## Study The Bible

☐ Read 1 Corinthians 14:33, Ephesians 2:13-14, Romans 5:1, and Philippians 4:6-7. Answer these questions, by writing the correct Bible reference on each line.

1. Which verse tells about peace with God because we know Jesus as Savior?

_____

2. Which verse tells us that God is the Author of Peace?_____

3. Which Scripture tells us that Jesus is our peace?_____

## Think About This

☐ Does knowing God personally give you peace inside?

_____   _____

Parent or adult signature       Date

# The Island Of Lost Treasures ✶ WEEK 23

Soon, some of the crew came running to see the wonderful treasures. Everyone was excited and jumping for joy as more and more treasure was discovered. Even some of the island natives gathered to see what was going on. John stood back and watched the happy crew. He wished he could remember this moment forever.

**The joy God gives to His children is for *now* and *forever!***

## Memory Verse

☐ Say Psalm 16:11 again. See page 27.

## Study The Verse

☐ Underline Psalm 16:11 in your Bible.

☐ Where do we find fullness of joy (complete joy)?_____

## Study The Bible

☐ Read each Bible story. Tell what was the reason for joy in each story.

The Lost Sheep (Luke 15:3-7): _____

The Lost Coin (Luke 15:8-10): _____

The Lost Son (Luke 15:11-24): _____

☐ Reread Luke 15:7 and 10. What is the reason for joy in these verses?_____

☐ Define the word repent. Use a dictionary. _____

_____

## Something To Do

☐ Write a short poem about the joy God gives. Use free verse or a rhyme.

_____          _____
Parent or adult signature                      Date

Everyone was enjoying the wonderful discovery of hidden treasure. The more John and Isabel, the captain and their father, and the crew dug, the more treasure they found. They were all enjoying another special treasure — being together in each other's presence.

**There are many great treasures in the Bible, but the greatest treasure is knowing Jesus Christ as your personal Savior and enjoying His presence in your life.**

## Memory Verse

☐ *". . . and, lo, I am with you always, even unto the end of the world."*
Matthew 28:20b

## Study The Verse

☐ What is Jesus' promise in Matthew 28:20b? _____

_____

☐ Underline Matthew 28:20b in your Bible.

## Study The Bible

Since Jesus is not with us in body, He is with us in Spirit. His presence with us is called the Holy Spirit.

☐ Read John 14:15-20. Write one important fact found in these verses. _____

_____

☐ Read Isaiah 41:10. God makes a promise. What is it? _____

_____

## Think About This

☐ Look at a map of the world and think of the farthest place on earth that you could possibly go. Remember that Jesus will be with you even there. Whenever you are sad or afraid, remember Jesus is right beside you to help you and give you strength. Now memorize Isaiah 41:10.

_____    _____
Parent or adult signature          Date

All too soon it was time to leave the island and continue on the voyage. On board the *Explorer* was a chest full of treasure. John and Isabel wondered if there would be more exciting adventures on this voyage. Would they discover a new land? Would they return safely home?

You have discovered God's treasures of love, joy, peace, and His presence. Don't stop now. Continue to study God's Word and you will find many more treasures. But remember, all spiritual treasures begin with knowing Jesus Christ as personal Savior.

## Memory Verse

☐ Say Colossians 2:3 again. See page 25.

## Study The Verse

☐ Define these words. Use a dictionary.

wisdom _____

knowledge _____

## Study The Bible

☐ Match the correct verse with the treasure God promises to us when we accept Jesus as Savior.

Matthew 28:20b　　　　　Love

John 14:27　　　　　　　Joy

Romans 5:8　　　　　　　Peace

Psalm 16:11　　　　　　　God's presence

## Think About This

☐ God has many wonderful things planned for you. Seek the treasure in His Word, ask Him to help you obey Him and do what He wants you to do.

_____　　_____

Parent or adult signature　　　　　Date

After their adventure on the Island of Lost Treasures, John and Isabel realized the voyage was half over for them! What thrilling memories they had to take home with them, and they hoped the second half of the trip would be as wonderful as the first!

Christians have more than knowledge **and memories of Jesus Christ. Christians have Jesus Christ with them every day. We have God's presence with us all the time. We have God's peace with us all the time.**

## Memory Verse

☐ Say Matthew 28:20b and John 14:27 again.
See pages 31 and 29.

## Study The Verse

☐ Answer these questions from Matthew 28:20b and John 14:27.

1. How often is Jesus with you? _____

2. What does Jesus give you? _____

3. What does Jesus tell you not to do? _____

## Study The Bible

☐ Read each verse below. What do these verses tell us about peace?

Isaiah 26:3 _____

Philippians 4:7 _____

## Something To Do

☐ Say these verses again until you know them by heart:

☐ Colossians 2:3

☐ Psalm 16:11

☐ Romans 5:8

_____      _____
Parent or adult signature                              Date

# MAKING REPAIRS

Soon after the ship left The Island of Lost Treasures, Isabel disobeyed one of the rules of the ship. She knew she was not to open the window during the storm, but she wanted to see what was going on! The water rushed into the cabin as the giant waves hit the ship. Although Isabel tried to close the window immediately, the water flooded the floor of the cabin by the time she finally got the window closed and locked. Everything else was soaking wet too, and the captain said they would have to stop at a nearby island for repairs. Of course, having to stop for repairs delayed their trip.

Isabel felt terrible. She went to the captain and asked for forgiveness. He kindly forgave her and she promised to not disobey the rules again. Then she went back to her soggy cabin, and searched through all her papers until she found the list of the ship's rules.

"I'd better study these again," she said to herself. "I don't want to make any more mistakes."

Christians make mistakes, too. Remember that we have a kind, loving heavenly Father Who is ready to forgive us when we come to Him and are truly sorry for our sins. Check your own life and make any necessary repairs. Do you need to ask for God's forgiveness for anything?

Isabel found out that her disobedience also hurt other people. The water flooding her cabin dripped down into the cabin below, soaking the crewmen's clothing and beds. The captain said the necessary repairs to Isabel's cabin would cost a lot of money, and of course delay the trip by several days.

But despite her disobedience, Isabel also discovered forgiveness when she asked for it. The captain and her father forgave her and she knew God forgave her too. She felt clean inside.

**Remember, when you are disobedient God is ready to forgive you and make you clean inside again. He will also help you to do the right thing next time.**

## Memory Verse

☐ *"If we confess our sins, He is faithful and just to forgive us our sins, and to cleanse us from all unrighteousness."*

1 John 1:9

## Study The Verse

☐ Define these words. Use a dictionary.

confess _____

unrighteousness _____

## Study The Bible

When we sin we should confess our sins and tell God we are sorry. David sinned. He coveted a married woman and arranged for her husband to be killed so he could marry her.

☐ Read Psalm 51. This is David's prayer of repentance to God after he sinned. Underline verses 2 and 10 in your Bible. What does David ask God to do in these verses? _____

_____

## Think About This

☐ When you do something wrong, does it hurt anyone? Does it hurt God? What should you do when you've done something wrong?

_____     _____

Parent or adult signature                        Date

# Making Repairs  WEEK 28

"I'LL DO MY BEST!"

Isabel renewed her commitment to the trip and to the captain. She would do her best. But if she made mistakes, she knew that there was forgiveness and help. She was happy to be part of the *Explorer* crew.

**A Christian's first priority is his commitment to God. God loves us and He wants our complete love. Even when we make mistakes and do wrong, God loves us and He will forgive us.**

## Memory Verse

☐ Say Mark 12:30 again. See page 9.

## Study The Verse

☐ Fill in the blanks.

*"And thou shalt _____ the LORD thy _____ with all thy _____ , and with all thy _____ , and with all thy _____ , and with all thy _____ : This is the first _____ ."* Mark 12:30

## Study The Bible

☐ Read about Stephen in Acts 7:54-60. Stephen loved Jesus so much that he was willing to die for Him, and he did!

Answer these questions.

1. Who did Stephen see as he was dying? (see verses 55, 56) _____

2. What was Stephen's attitude to those who hurt him? (see verse 60) _____

_____

## Think About This

☐ Do you think Stephen loved God with all his heart, soul, mind, and strength? How much do you love God? Do you love God as much as Stephen did?

_____  _____
Parent or adult signature          Date

# Making Repairs  WEEK 29

Father asked John to go to their cabin and get his maps. He gave John specific instructions on how to roll the maps and tie them together. But when John found the maps, he thought it would be easier to just carry the maps without rolling and tying them like his father said. However, John obeyed and did exactly as his father said. "Thank you, John," his father said when John returned with the maps. "Thank you for rolling and tying the maps as I told you. The maps could have been ruined if you had not followed my directions." When John heard that, he was glad he had obeyed!

**God has given you parents to teach you and guide you in life. Parents can teach you the right way to do things and the right way to behave. Listen to your parents. This is one of God's commands. (See page 17.)**

## Memory Verse

☐ *"Children, obey your parents in the Lord: for this is right. Honour thy father and mother; which is the first commandment with promise; That it may be well with thee, and thou mayest live long on the earth."*
Ephesians 6:1-3

## Study The Verse

☐ In the verses above, put a box around the word "obey." Underline the words "in the Lord." Circle the words "for this is right."

☐ What is the first commandment *with promise?* _____

What is the promise? _____

## Study The Bible

☐ Read the verses below. Write what each verse says in your own words.

Proverbs 23:22 _____

Proverbs 4:1 _____

## Something To Do

☐ Make a list of at least three reasons for obeying your parents.

_____  _____
Parent or adult signature          Date

Isabel wanted the people in the next cabin to know she cared about them, but she was too shy. One day the people next door became ill. "I know what I'll do," thought Isabel. "I will take dinner to them. Then they will know I care."

God wants us to love others. This is a very important command God wants us to obey. This brings glory to His name. Remember, God loves your relatives, your friends, your neighbors — and everyone!

## Memory Verse

☐ *"And the second is like, namely this, Thou shalt love thy neighbor as thyself. There is none other commandment greater than these."*

Mark 12:31

## Study The Verse

☐ The first commandment is to love God (Remember Mark 12:30, see page 9.). What does Jesus say is the second commandment? _____

_____

## Study The Bible

☐ Read about the Good Samaritan in Luke 10:30-37. In what four ways did the Samaritan show love to the hurt man?

_____    _____

_____    _____

## Something To Do

☐ Do something nice for a teacher, neighbor, friend, or someone at church to show them you love them. You may bake cookies, do yard work, make a gift, send a nice card, write a poem, or paint a picture. There are many little ways too, that we can show people we love them every day. Try to show a different person each day this week that you love them, by something you do.

_____    _____
Parent or adult signature                Date

# Making Repairs  WEEK 31

An older boy on the crew was always picking on John — calling him names and making John do his work. One day John had the opportunity to get even with this nasty boy, but then John remembered the ship's rule: "Don't hurt one another." So John tried hard to be kind and loving to the boy even though he was mean and nasty.

**God tells us in the Bible to *love* our enemies and people who do bad things to us. This is very hard to do! In fact, it is impossible to love our enemies without God's help, but God will help us if we ask Him.**

## Memory Verse

☐ *"But I say unto you, Love your enemies, bless them that curse you, do good to them that hate you, and pray for them which despitefully use you, and persecute you."*

Matthew 5:44

## Study The Verse

☐ Circle the four commands found in Matthew 5:44.

## Study The Bible

☐ Read the following Scripture passages. Match each one to the correct thought.

| | |
|---|---|
| Ephesians 6:1-3 | Love your enemies |
| Matthew 5:43-45 | Love others |
| Mark 12:31 | Love God |
| Mark 12:30 | Love your parents |

## Something To Do

☐ Do you have enemies? Write their names at right. Then pray for them each day for one week. Ask God to help you love your enemies. See if you feel any differently toward them after you have prayed for them for one week.

Check off each day you pray in the boxes below.

_____    _____
Parent or adult signature                    Date

Finally the repairs needed as a result of Isabel's disobedience were made, and the *Explorer* set out to sea. Isabel tackled her chores with a happy spirit. The good relationship she had with the captain and her father had been damaged by her disobedience, but after she asked for forgiveness, everyone was happy again.

**When we sin, God wants us to tell Him about it and ask His forgiveness. This is what is meant by "confessing our sins." Confessing our sins repairs a broken relationship between us and God.**

## Memory Verse

☐ Say 1 John 1:9 again. See page 35.

## Study The Verse

☐ Write 1 John 1:9 in your own words. _____

_____

☐ Underline 1 John 1:9 in your Bible.

## Study The Bible

☐ Read about Peter denying Christ in Mark 14:29-31 and 66-72. Answer these questions.

1. What did Peter do? (see verses 68, 70, 71) _____

2. How do you think Peter felt after he denied Christ? (see verse 72) _____

3. Do you think Jesus forgave him? _____

## Think About This

☐ Do you need to confess anything to God? If so, just follow these simple steps:

1. Tell God you are sorry for what you did wrong.
2. Ask Him to forgive you.
3. Ask Him to help you not do wrong.
4. Thank God for forgiving you because of Jesus' death and resurrection.

_____     _____
Parent or adult signature                     Date

John and Isabel wanted to do their best on this voyage, but there were times when they just did not understand what to do. Today they were to "swab the deck," but they didn't know what that meant. Then the captain explained that to "swab the deck" means to wash the deck with a pail of water and a mop or scrub brush, and then the captain showed John and Isabel how to swab the decks themselves.

**God doesn't just give us rules to live by and then leave us on our own to try to figure out what to do. God is personally with us all the time to help us and to guide us to do the right thing.**

## Memory Verse

☐ *"I will instruct thee and teach thee in the way which thou shalt go: I will guide thee with mine eye."*
Psalm 32:8

## Study The Verse

☐ Who is speaking in Psalm 32:8?_____

☐ Find the two words in the puzzle which mean almost the same thing. Fill in the sections that have a dot. Then in the verse above circle the words you find in the puzzle.

INSTRUCT TEACH

## Study The Bible

☐ Read John 1:1-12. Who are these verses talking about?

Jesus is called the  ___ ___ R ___  and the  ___ ___ G ___ ___  in these verses.

## Think About This

☐ Jesus is our light. He is the way to God. He is our guide and our helper in all we do. Each morning you should ask Jesus to guide you to do the right things that day.

_____     _____
Parent or adult signature                    Date

John and Isabel stood on deck and looked out over the ocean. It had been a long time since they had seen land, and they wondered if they would ever see it again. Would they discover the New Land or would they sail on endlessly? But although John and Isabel didn't know what was going to happen next, they knew they could trust their captain to sail the ship in the right direction.

That's the way it is with God too. Even though we don't know what is ahead, God is in control of our lives and He will work out the best plans for each person who is committed to Him.

## Memory Verse

☐ Say Psalm 32:8 again. See page 41.

## Study The Verse

☐ Underline Psalm 32:8 in your Bible.

☐ Write what this verse means to you._____

_____

_____

## Study The Bible

☐ Read each verse. Match each verse to the correct thought.

Psalm 48:14          God is our Lamp

2 Samuel 22:29       God is our Guide

Proverbs 8:20        God is our Leader

## Something To Do

☐ Say these verses again.

☐ 1 John 1:9

☐ Mark 12:30, 31

☐ Ephesians 6:1-3

☐ Matthew 5:44

_____     _____

Parent or adult signature            Date

# EXPLORING THE NEW LAND

LAND HO!

After the exciting treasure hunt and stop for repairs, the voyage seemed to drag on forever. They had sailed for weeks without seeing any land or other ships. The crew was very tired, and food was running low.

Then one morning John and Isabel were awakened by a loud commotion outside their cabin.

"Land Ho! Land Ho!" an excited crewman yelled at the top of his voice. Everyone gathered to see what all the excitement was about. There on the horizon was a faint image of land. "The captain was right!" shouted John. "There is a new land!"

The captain estimated it would take at least two days to reach the shore of the new land they had discovered. The children's father pulled out his map paper and got ready to chart the new discovery.

What would they find in the new land? No one had ever come this far before! A little fear was mixed in with John and Isabel's excitement. But no matter what happened John and Isabel trusted the captain to lead them in exploring the new land.

Just as John and Isabel are trusting the captain to help them explore the new land, you can trust God to help you explore His Word, the Bible and find many wonderful "treasures" in it.

# Exploring The New Land

John and Isabel beamed with delight. How thrilling it was to be a part of the *Explorer* crew! As crew members they shared in the treasure and new discoveries. They were rich in many ways because they were part of the *Explorer* crew!

As Christians, we share in God's treasures because we are His children. We find these treasures by reading and studying God's Word, the Bible, and by doing what God wants us to do.

## Memory Verse

☐ *"The Spirit itself beareth witness with our spirit, that we are the children of God: And if children, then heirs; heirs of God, and joint-heirs with Christ;"*

Romans 8:16-17a

## Study The Verse

☐ Define these words. Use a dictionary.

heir _____

witness _____

☐ Answer these questions.

1. What does the Holy Spirit tell us? _____

_____

2. We are _____ - _____ with Christ.

## Study The Bible

☐ Read 1 John 5:11-13. What can those who believe in Jesus know for sure? (see verse 13)

_____

Read John 14:1-3. What is Jesus preparing for those who believe in Him?

_____

## Think About This

☐ You can share in all that God has when you are His child. To become God's child, just confess your sins, ask Jesus to forgive you, and believe on Jesus as your Savior.

_____     _____
Parent or adult signature                  Date

With only one day to go before reaching the new land, the captain and crew could see a storm brewing in the distance. They hoped the ship could make it to land before the storm hit, but by evening the storm was upon them and the high winds and waves tossed the ship to and fro.

As the ship rocked back and forth the children clung to their father in fear, but he assured them of the captain's ability to handle the *Explorer*, even in this terrible storm.

**Sometimes "storms" come into our lives and we are afraid. Our storms can be bad or sad things that happen to us, or things that make us afraid, like staying alone, losing someone or something we love, not doing well on a test, or being blamed for something you didn't do. When these "storms" happen, we need to remember to trust in our Father in heaven and to not be afraid.**

## Memory Verse

☐ *"What time I am afraid, I will trust in Thee."*
Psalm 56:3

## Study The Verse

☐ What should you do when you are afraid?_____

☐ Circle the word in the verse above that means God.

## Study The Bible

☐ Read Matthew 8:23-27. Answer these questions.

1. Why were the disciples afraid?_____

2. What did Jesus do? _____

## Something To Do

☐ Make a poster for your room. Write Psalm 56:3 on a large piece of paper. Draw or cut out a picture of Jesus and put on the poster. Then draw a picture of yourself next to Jesus. Or glue a picture of yourself next to Jesus. Put the poster up to remind you that Jesus is with you all the time and you can trust in Him when you are afraid, and all the time!

_____     _____
Parent or adult signature                Date

# Exploring The New Land  WEEK 37

Finally the storm was over. The damage to the ship was minor compared to the intensity of the storm. Without the captain's great knowledge of the ship and storms, the *Explorer* would likely have been driven off course or dashed to pieces upon the coral reef. John and Isabel were glad they had trusted their lives to the captain.

**Have you trusted Jesus Christ with your life? He can give you peace in the midst of the "storms" that come into your life, and bring you safely home to heaven to live with Him forever.**

## Memory Verse

☐ Say John 14:27 again. See page 29.

## Study The Verse

☐ Jesus tells us not to let our hearts be _____ or _____ . What does Jesus give us? _____ .

## Study The Bible

☐ Read Psalms 27:1; 56:4; 118:6; and Hebrews 13:6. Summarize what these verses mean to you.

_____

_____

_____

_____

_____

☐ Underline these verses in your Bible.

## Think About This

☐ If God is with you, is there anything of which you should be afraid? (Circle one)

     YES             NO

_____  _____
Parent or adult signature           Date

# Exploring The New Land  WEEK 38

At last the ship drew near the shore of the new land. The crew yelled out, "Hoorah!" and quickly all but a few of the people on board went ashore.

Oh, what wonderful things they found. All kinds of delicious, exotic fruits were growing wild. Everyone ate to their heart's content. What a wonderful new land they had found!

Jesus wants us to produce fruit for Him. Producing fruit means to do things which help other people believe in Jesus as their Savior. The only way that a Christian can produce fruit is if he or she is following, or abiding in, Jesus and doing God's will.

## Memory Verse

☐ *"I am the vine, ye are the branches: He that abideth in Me, and I in him, the same bringeth forth much fruit: for without Me ye can do nothing."*

John 15:5

## Study The Verse

☐ Check the best meaning for "abide."

☐ to share your troubles with Christ;
☐ to forget all about Jesus

☐ to study about Jesus
☐ to follow Jesus and obey Him

☐ Can we produce spiritual fruit in our lives without Jesus? (Circle one)
    YES          NO

☐ Circle the part of the verse that says this.

## Study The Bible

☐ Read John 15:1-8. Answer these questions.

1. What happens to the person not abiding in Christ? (see verse 6)_____

2. When is God the Father glorified? (see verse 8)_____

## Something To Do

☐ Write a prayer to God. In your prayer tell Jesus you want to abide in Him and produce spiritual fruit.

_____   _____
Parent or adult signature        Date

The *Explorer* crew shared the wonderful adventure of discovering the new land together. The entire crew had become very close. They were like one big family who enjoys being together and doing things with one another.

**When you belong to Jesus Christ, you become a part of His family. In His family you have brothers and sisters in Christ. Your brothers and sisters in Christ are also heirs of God and joint-heirs with Christ. Do you share spiritual things with your Christian family?**

## Memory Verse

☐ Say Romans 8:16-17a again. See page 44.

## Study The Verse

☐ Underline these verses in your Bible.

☐ Tell in your own words what it means to you to be God's heir? _____

_____

## Study The Bible

☐ Read Philippians 2:1-5. These verses tell how we should treat our brothers and sisters in Christ. Fill in the blanks.

*Be ___ ___ ___ e - m ___ ___ ___ ___ d , having the same _____ , being of one accord, of one*

*_____ . (verse 2) Let each esteem other(s) better than _____ . (verse 3) Let this*

*_____ be in you, which was also in _____ _____ : (verse 5)*

## Think About This

☐ When you know Jesus as your personal Savior, you are not just a friend of God, but you are His own child! Have you become God's child by receiving Jesus as your Savior?

_____      _____
Parent or adult signature                              Date

The Captain warned all the crew members to stay close together and near the shore. "There may be hidden dangers," he explained. "So do not wander off by yourself."

John was tempted to go exploring on his own, but decided it would not be the best thing to do. He was glad he was obedient when he learned of another crew member who left the group, fell in a hole and broke his leg.

**We are all tempted to do things we should not do. God can help us to say "no" to temptation and do the right thing.**

## Memory Verse

☐ *"There hath no temptation taken you but such as is common to man: but God is faithful, who will not suffer you to be tempted above that ye are able; but will with the temptation also make a way to escape, that ye may be able to bear it."*

1 Corinthians 10:13

## Study The Verse

☐ List some temptations which are common to you and to other children your age.

_____  _____  _____

_____  _____  _____

☐ Circle the part of the verse which tells you what God is able to do for you when you are tempted.

## Study The Bible

☐ Read in Matthew 4:1-11 about when Jesus was tempted. What did Jesus use against the temptation?

Unscramble the letters below to find the answer:

hTe _____ orWd _____ fo _____ oGd _____

## Something To Do

☐ Write a short story about someone your age who is tempted to do something wrong. Have the young person in your story choose to trust God and do the right thing. Share your story with someone else.

_____  _____
Parent or adult signature                    Date

As the *Explorer* crew walked together along the shoreline, they were met by several natives. Were they friendly? Would they hurt the crew?

John and Isabel stood behind their father. The captain moved toward the natives and began to use sign language to speak with them. The children had trusted the captain in the storm. They would trust him to make friends with the natives. Soon the natives offered the captain food and wooden tools. It looked like they had found friends in this new land.

**Remember you can trust God in any situation, no matter if it is a happy, friendly situation, or an unfriendly one!**

## Memory Verse

☐ Say Psalm 56:3 again. See page 45.

## Study The Verse

☐ Underline this verse in your Bible.

☐ Write about one instance when you were afraid and trusted God. What happened?

_____

_____

## Study The Bible

☐ Read Daniel, chapter 3. Answer these questions.

1. What did Shadrach, Meshach, and Abednego have to fear?_____

2. What did God do for them?_____

3. Who was with them in the furnace? Who is with you all the time to help you when you are afraid?_____

## Think About This

☐ God is great and powerful. He is with you all the time to take care of you and guide you. He is on your side if you belong to Him!

_____     _____
Parent or adult signature                    Date

Soon the entire *Explorer* crew greeted the natives. John and Isabel met some native children their age. They tried to communicate and exchanged a few trinkets with each other. The children knew how important their behavior was at this time. They had the opportunity and responsibility to spread good will from their country to the people of this new land.

**Christians have the responsibility of telling the world about their Savior, Jesus Christ. How we act makes a difference in whether other people will want to accept Jesus as their Savior.**

## Memory Verse

☐ *"Let your light so shine before men, that they may see your good works, and glorify your Father which is in heaven."*

Matthew 5:16

## Study The Verse

☐ What will people do when they see your shining light and good works, according to Matthew 5:16?

_____

## Study The Bible

☐ Read about Jesus' good works in the two passages below and tell what Jesus did.

Luke 9:12-17 _____

Matthew 8:5-13 _____

## Something To Do

☐ Write one thing you will do today to let your light shine for Jesus:

_____

_____   _____
Parent or adult signature                          Date

# Exploring The New Land  WEEK 43

After weeks of exploring this exciting new land and helping their father make maps, it was time for John and Isabel and the *Explorer* to leave for home.

The natives had learned much from the friendly strangers, and were very sad to see the crew leave. Long after the *Explorer* left the shore, the natives stood on the sand waving to their departing friends. On the ship, John and Isabel waved until the new land was only a thin line on the horizon. They would miss their new friends but they were excited to be on the way home too!

**Are you a successful witness for Jesus Christ? Are your friends glad to know you because you shine for Jesus?**

## Memory Verse

- [ ] Say Matthew 5:16 again. See page 51.

## Study The Verse

- [ ] Underline Matthew 5:16 in your Bible.

- [ ] What does this verse mean to you? _____

_____

## Study The Bible

- [ ] Read about someone who let his light shine for Jesus. Read Acts 8:26-39. Who was the man? What did he do?

_____

## Something To Do

- [ ] Say these verses again until you know them by heart:
  - [ ] Psalm 56:3
  - [ ] 1 Corinthians 10:13
  - [ ] Romans 8:16, 17b
  - [ ] John 15:5

_____  _____

Parent or adult signature        Date

# WELCOME HOME

Loaded with fruits and trinkets from the new land, the *Explorer* was on its way home. This exciting voyage was almost over. John and Isabel had learned much on this trip. They had learned about obedience, responsibility, commitment and about being part of a ship's crew. They had dug for buried treasure — and found some! They had shared in the discovery of a new land, and their father had updated his maps. It had been a fruitful trip, indeed!

Every minute of hard work had been worth it. "How wonderful it will be to arrive home and share our adventures with Mother and our friends," said John. Isabel agreed. "It will be fun to tell our friends about our adventures too."

You are almost to the end of your study in this book. You have worked hard learning God's Word and exploring the treasures in His Word. Now you have much to share about Christ with your family and friends.

The Explorer was getting nearer to its home port. John and Isabel could see the lights in the harbor. "We'll be home soon," said Isabel. "Home — that word sure sounds wonderful, doesn't it, John?"
"It sure does," John agreed.

As a Christian, your life on earth is not the end for you. Heaven is your final home! Although you want your life to be happy and enjoyable, and you want to live a long time, and do many things during your lifetime, always remember that this life is only the beginning. If you know Jesus as your Savior, you will spend eternity with Jesus in your heavenly home.

## Memory Verse

☐ *"In my Father's house are many mansions: if it were not so, I would have told you. I go to prepare a place for you."*

John 14:2

## Study The Verse

☐ What place is Jesus talking about in the verse above?

____ ____ ____ V ____ ____

☐ Underline this verse in your Bible.

## Study The Bible

☐ Read John 14:1-6 in your Bible. Answer these questions.
1. Which verse tells that Jesus cared how His disciples felt? _____
2. Jesus assured His disciples that He would come for them. Which verse tells about this?

_____

3. Verse 6 tells us the only way to get to heaven. Fill in the blanks:

____ ____ S ____ ____   is the   ____ ____ ____

## Think About This

☐ What do you think heaven will be like?

_____     _____
Parent or adult signature                    Date

The ship sailed closer and closer to shore. Soon John and Isabel could see their mother and friends on shore. They waved as hard as they could. Soon they would be home in the presence of their family and friends.

In the Bible, Paul wrote that he wanted to be in Jesus' presence. Paul wanted to be with Jesus in heaven. As Christians, we should also want to be with Jesus in heaven when our life on earth is completed.

## Memory Verse

☐ *"We are . . . willing rather to be absent from the body, and to be present with the Lord."*
2 Corinthians 5:8

## Study The Verse

☐ What does "absent from the body" mean? _____

☐ What does "present with the Lord" mean? _____

## Study The Bible

☐ Read 2 Corinthians 5:1-10. Answer these questions.

1. What is your body called in verse 1? _____

2. Verse 9 says that the most important thing for you to do is to please God. Verse 10 explains one reason for this. What is it? _____

## Think About This

☐ When you stand before Christ, will He be pleased with how you lived your life?

_____     _____
Parent or adult signature                         Date

# Welcome Home  WEEK 46

The magnificent *Explorer* finally docked. John and Isabel ran down the gangplank and into their mother's arms. What joy and excitement! They were home at last!

**Someday we will be home too — home with our Lord and Savior Jesus Christ in heaven forever!**

## Memory Verse

☐ Say John 14:2 again. See page 54.

## Study The Verse

☐ Who is Jesus' Father?_____

☐ What is Jesus preparing for us?_____

## Study The Bible

☐ Read 1 Thessalonians 4:13-18 and Matthew 24:36-42. Describe what it will be like when Jesus returns to take those who believe in Him to heaven.

_____

_____

_____

_____

_____

_____

_____

## Something To Do

☐ Draw a picture of what it could be like when Jesus returns, or write a short creative story about the reaction of people here on earth when Jesus returns.

_____     _____
Parent or adult signature                        Date

At home John and Isabel bombarded their mother with interesting descriptions of their exciting adventures. They showed her the jewels they had found and the trinkets from their native friends in the new land. Mother listened intently to all of their tales of adventure. "I feel like I was there with you," she said. "I am so glad you had a safe voyage and are home at last."

**Christians have the responsibility to tell others about our wonderful Savior, Jesus Christ. Have you ever shared your experiences with Jesus Christ with someone else?**

## Memory Verse

☐ *"And He said unto them, Go ye into all the world, and preach the gospel to every creature."*
Mark 16:15

## Study The Verse

☐ Circle these key words in the verse above:
go, world, preach, gospel, creature

## Study The Bible

☐ Read Romans 10:13-15, 17. Answer these questions.

1. What should we tell others? (see verse 13)_____

2. What does God call the feet of those who preach the gospel? (see verse 15)_____

3. Fill in the blanks: Faith cometh by _____ , and hearing by the _____ of _____ . (verse 17)

## Something To Do

☐ Explain to someone (a parent, friend, sister, brother or other person) how to become a Christian. Ask them if they would like to be a Christian, and pray with them to accept Jesus as their personal Savior.

_____    _____
Parent or adult signature                         Date

# Welcome Home  WEEK 48

It was very late when Mother tucked her tired children into bed. The voyage had been fantastic, yet their own beds felt so good to John and Isabel. As John and Isabel lay in their own beds they thought about their trip and knew they would not have traded the experience for anything. But it certainly was nice to be home!

God plans an abundant life for each of His children as they trust in Him, yet it will be wonderful to be at home in heaven with Jesus someday!

## Memory Verse

☐ Say 2 Corinthians 5:8 again. See page 55.

## Study The Verse

☐ Fill in the blanks.

"We are _____ rather to be _____ from the _____ , and to be _____ with the _____ ."   2 Corinthians 5:8

## Study The Bible

☐ Look up the following references. In each case, fill in the chart below.

| Reference | Who died? | Do you think he went to heaven? | Why? |
|---|---|---|---|
| Matthew 27:3-5 | | | |
| Mark 6:22-29 | | | |

## Think About This

☐ Do you get excited when people talk about heaven? You should, if you believe in Jesus, heaven will be your eternal home!

_____   _____
Parent or adult signature              Date

When John and Isabel awoke the next morning they found the house full of interested friends. Their friends asked a multitude of questions, and John and Isabel greatly enjoyed sharing with them the experiences of their voyage.

**Christians should enjoy sharing Jesus Christ with their friends. Sharing Jesus Christ with others is a privilege and a responsibility we have as Christians.**

## Memory Verse

☐ Say Mark 16:15 again. See page 57.

## Study The Verse

☐ Underline Mark 16:15 in your Bible.

## Study The Bible

☐ Read John 3:16, John 3:36, John 1:12, Romans 3:23, Romans 6:23, Romans 5:8 and Acts 16:31. Summarize the gospel message found in these verses.

_____

_____

_____

_____

_____

_____

_____

## Think About This

☐ Think of a friend who needs to know Jesus as their personal Savior. Using the steps above, tell them about Jesus and how they can accept Him as Savior.

_____     _____
Parent or adult signature                Date

# Welcome Home  WEEK 50

As the children continued to talk about their trip, their mother soon realized what a wonderful leader and friend the captain had been to her children. He had taught them many things.

**Jesus is our Friend, our Leader, our Teacher and our Good Shepherd.**

## Memory Verse

☐ 1. *"The Lord is my Shepherd: I shall not want.*
2. *He maketh me to lie down in green pastures: He leadeth me beside the still waters.*
3. *He restoreth my soul: He leadeth me in the paths of righteousness for His Name's sake."*
Psalm 23:1-3

## Study The Verse

☐ Underline these verses in your Bible.

> CAPTAIN:
> JESUS
> CHRIST

## Study The Bible

☐ Answer these questions about Psalm 23:1-3.

1. The phrase "I shall not want" in verse 1 means that because the Lord is your Shepherd you have everything you need. Name two things that God does for you:

_____

_____

2. Verses 2 and 3 tell some places the Lord leads us. What do each of the locations in the Psalm represent:

Green pastures: _____

Still waters: _____

Paths of righteousness: _____

## Think About This

☐ The Lord is your Shepherd and Guide through life, and when your life is over, you will spend eternity with Him!

_____     _____
Parent or adult signature                    Date

THE CAPTAIN WAS GREAT!

While they were on the voyage, the captain led his crew to make new discoveries. He cared for his crew and protected them during a terrible storm, and he taught John and Isabel many things.

John and Isabel loved the captain very much and spoke long and lovingly about him to their mother and friends.

**Jesus Christ leads us, cares for us, protects us and teaches us. Praise His name! We shall live with Him forever!**

## Memory Verse

4. *"Yea, though I walk through the valley of the shadow of death, I will fear no evil for Thou art with me; Thy rod and Thy staff they comfort me.*
5. *Thou preparest a table before me in the presence of mine enemies: Thou anointest my head with oil; my cup runneth over.*
6. *Surely goodness and mercy shall follow me all the days of my life: and I will dwell in the house of the Lord for ever."*
   Psalm 23:4-6

## Study The Verse

Underline these verses in your Bible.

## Study The Bible

Answer these questions about Psalm 23:4-6.

1. Why should you fear no evil? (verse 4)_____

2. Where will you live forever? (verse 6)_____

## Something To Do

Make a poster of Psalm 23. Cut pictures from magazines to illustrate all of Psalm 23. Write the verses next to the pictures. Put your poster up in your room to remind you of Jesus, your Good Shepherd Who loves you and cares for you.

_____     _____
Parent or adult signature                    Date

The *Explorer* would soon be leaving on another voyage. John and Isabel went to the harbor to say "good-bye" to their friend, the captain, and to thank him for a wonderful voyage. With tears in their eyes, they said "good-bye." They hated to leave their wonderful leader. "We hope to see you again someday," they said. "You will always have a special place in our hearts!"

**Be thankful that you can never be separated from your leader, Jesus Christ. Jesus is with you always, and you will spend eternity with Him in heaven if you belong to Him.**

## Memory Verse

☐ Say all of Psalm 23 again. See pages 60 and 61.

## Study The Verse

☐ Circle the phrases or sentences that mean the most to you in Psalm 23 on pages 60 and 61.

## Study The Bible

☐ Read John 10:1-18. Who is the Good Shepherd? _____

## Something To Do

☐ Say each of these verses until you know them by heart.

    ☐ John 14:2

    ☐ 2 Corinthians 5:8

    ☐ Mark 16:15

_____   _____

Parent or adult signature        Date

# CONTINUE ON YOUR JOURNEY

On your exciting sea voyage with John and Isabel, you have learned how to explore God's Word, the Bible, and how to live the way Jesus wants you to.

Your adventure in God's Word is not over. Here are some easy ways to keep on exploring God's Word and living for Jesus:

☐ Keep exploring God's Word by reading some of the Bible each day. Read the book of John in the New Testament first.

☐ Go to Sunday school and church every Sunday. Church is where we worship God and learn more about Him.

☐ Learn a Bible verse each week. Review the verses in this book. Other verses to memorize are: Revelation 3:20, Psalm 4:3b, Romans 8:28, Isaiah 41:10, 1 John 4:7a, and 1 John 4:19.

☐ Try to obey Jesus by doing the right things every day. Obey your parents. Do your best at school. Do your chores without being asked. Be kind and helpful to your family.

☐ Tell other people about Jesus and help them accept Him as their personal Savior. Just use these simple ABCs:

    **A.** Admit you have done wrong things which are sinful.

    **B.** Believe Jesus died on the cross and came alive again so your sins can be forgiven.

    **C.** Call on Jesus in prayer to become your Savior.

**Let's get started on the greatest adventure of all: following Jesus !**